what

replaces

us

when

we

go

what replaces us when we go

Julie Doxsee

**Black Ocean**
Boston · Detroit · Chicago

Black Ocean
P.O. Box 52030
Boston, MA 02205
blackocean.org

Cover & Book Design by Nikkita Cohoon | nikkita.co

ISBN 978-1-939568-22-9

Library of Congress Cataloging-in-Publication Data

Names: Doxsee, Julie, author.
Title: What replaces us when we go / Julie Doxsee.
Description: Boston, MA : Black Ocean, [2017]
Identifiers: LCCN 2017048197 | ISBN 9781939568229 (pbk. : alk. paper)
Classification: LCC PS3604.O9545 A6 2017 | DDC 811/.6-dc23
LC record available at https://lccn.loc.gov/2017048197

FIRST EDITION

For ABCD & Joy

# CONTENTS

## JOY

## OH OH OH

## IN SEARCH OF FACES
## IN THE DEAD OF NIGHT

## ORPHANS

· · · · · ·

*But the fruit. What would become of the fruit? But man. What would become of man?*

—Edmond Jabès

# JOY

# MIDNIGHT

Clocks move the microphone
a piece of hourglass forgot

till the children choired it
from two hills away.  Whose eyes

blink through the wake-up
you can't talk face-to-face with

until crickets begin to fold
back into your mother's name?

By then she, shh, was
a sealed envelope tucked

into one of seven dunes . . .
Before you sever the sand

with a fire axe to find her,
pronounce the last two grains

as red as you can & wrap them
with gauze between a folded

photo of the cry we left out.

# NOON

One black cow coaxes ten boys
through the forest gate, twenty

sugar-shrunk lips blow kisses
to the stampede of cows left back.

The fattest taxi man in the city
laughs, goes ataraxic, snores

in the middle of a lunge headed right
for the sea.  This is where I die.

The herd's crusted eyes blink off flies
that leave moving holes in the white.

# THIS IS THE SUGAR

At noon there is one dog
sleepwalking her eight-puppy

pregnancy headfirst
into a glass wall, there is one

curled up fetal & nosing the
fly rags of the sugar spill.

This is the only sugar
fusing my mouth shut like

holidays. This is the only time
I wrap myself in a flag, throw

dead flies in the air & bat them
into the black as they confetti.

# COCOONS

I pluck two cocoons
overgrowing the porch bulb

as pine needles stab my toes
by the hundred. *You are the lungs*

*of a man I know* I say
to the cocoons, then I cradle them

in my hand & take them
on a boat tour of the city

until the snow falls & the lit-up homes
on the shoreline distill into the trees

they once were. *I am going to teach*
*you things about trees* I say

to the cocoons, hyperventilating.

# BLACK SEA

A fly's vibration wakes up
cone-ear dogs the forest

wide & every morning
the same choir of howls

tears a vertical chute
in the mist & fills it

with throat-wet diamonds.
The wet bones we walk on

from inside feel not air but eyes
in the sharp ditches of white. Only

the white is not white it is raccoons
& where your teeth should be

there are no teeth, there are only
footprints under which the animals sleep.

# AMUSEMENT PARKS

Every morning at 6 you say

*behind your eye there is*
*a picture of amusement*

*parks: ten steel monsters*
*rollercoastering the deep*

*pine woods & a thousand pink*
*sugar clouds melting the black*

*into one concentrated corner*
*where only you are visible.*

I know today we will exhume
tipped-over ferris wheels

long-buried by mud & drag them slowly
out to sea; with them we will drag

some sad songs, a bird nest,
the hardened minutes rusted

permanently onto the frame,
the holographic sticker

we stuck to a bolt the moment
we realized our gazes go to infinity

when we go without blinking,
& the rotating echo of

*behind your eye there is*
*a picture of amusement*

*parks: ten steel monsters*
*rollercoastering the deep*

*pine woods & a thousand pink*
*sugar clouds melting the black*

*into one concentrated corner*
*where only you are visible.*

# SUGAR

When I get up to stir
the pot, I catch the last

whiz its wing makes—
a film my two hands

press between two panes.
It's sunrise. I'm outside

& forgot to throw something
over my boobs. A little man

out here in the fog
sweeps up rotten arugula

the wild dogs cough up.
There is blood in poppy

shapes, a puppy licking glass—
blood freckles everywhere

like flung from the tips of a cut-
open hand. There's one empty

bird cage on the third stair.
The man stops sweeping

to draw on the cobblestone
with his air freshener in boob

shapes. Invisible. This is where I live.

# FOR AN EYE

As we trade fly wings
back and forth

your magic glasses
disintegrate. Now you see

only a sun & another sun
& another sun & another sun

& another sun & another sun
you've tracked all the way

from the North Pole
to my forest. This is distant.

A piece of sea turns
into an index finger & taps

the window, I throw
a mountain at it. The only

fire tower for miles
burns down &

salt-diamonds wash up
from old graves.

# SANCTUARIES UPROOT ACCORDING TO SILENCE

When the quiet unbites
a long photo noses up

like a silly muscle & there is
your eye masking over

as if you'd snared each
love like a tiny chip

of glass to keep under
your toy church where

a few crumbling letters
on a pew go stale, rotted

rakes booby-trap a vineless hole
in the garden waiting

for the rest of the
alphabet to swallow.

# A SUBTONE OF THE BLACK WOOD

Birds in the wood kill
a dying mermaid & I eat.

One day I ate a pile of giant
bird throats & left the bones—I stopped my handful

of fresh feathers on a dime below your earlobe where

a weathervane
can set off all the high-pitched

creatures you want dead.

So if you hear her, hold her
when you stand in the forest solo

first from the back with a
delicate hand & her smooth-scale

wanting-only-to-scream-that-way
will curve to you.

# BLUE HANDS

The death hoax your child
blues herself with

draws each claw from its
cloak for a wave

hither in the sexy sexy
void of a beauty

filled once with fat ankles
& the echo-surface of razors.

After the mother dies
her pieces of warm pie live

on on the kitchen counter.

# SOUNDS OF MEDICINE

Behind a loose door's
hinge-cricket obbligato, you notice

the spinal cord & on it
a layer of heel marks frowning, then

a baby paws the smoky noise
between him & the several up-down

suns grown over with sudden smudges
that make you shred your book

to woody pieces & think
*I've breastfed forever, but who?*

# LUNCH WITH 69

Talk awkward those middle
chapters of the new page

where a me-me vanishes
as broken teeth from childhood

push, finally, out of your shut
jaw, no matter what fourth

molar or other nerve
they drew need from. When you

look you'll find in tow a heart
that was raised a sponge

by its single parent, The Pig Toy.

# I F

Exactly one point five
percent of you is in love

with one point five percent
of whoever wandered into your

house like a slayer, took off
your outlet covers room by room

& flung them into the hurricane.
Each cracked socket you

can't see coaxes a lingering
*what now?* two blinking pairs

of eyes fill with hours.
For example, quiet

is a smoothed-out something
you bit down on to un-vibrate

your head, but a symphony came out & made
new shockwaves less ghosty than

the miniature integer you knew
by electrocution only.


If this be orthodox, a hollow man lifts
& fills with muscles shook

from a figure that was there
in her fist & freed a bit

with every gesture
toward the storm.

# WILD DUCTS & THE OWL BANG

Glass that will never agonize
out of my chest I did swallow

a large piece of. These
pectoral maneuvers, air-

mailed to the police
every six years, stay safe.

You know what I mean.
Sometimes you feel so

joybubbled it's illegal &
sometimes the agony

of a moon barbed with
bite marks needs a choir

of hooty sirens launching off
the mountain to match it.

# LITTLE EAGLE IN YOUR MIND

A man in a little eagle costume
cried, said *thank you*

*now murder my answer*
*behind the teeth.* A vacuum

came along, suctioned
from the sun a leftover lung

& soon an airplane
tethered to such

immaculate bisections
got fly-trapped there

where any man in a little eagle costume
would thin to vapor.

# ME

Somewhere someone gives a haircut to a baby goat and spells ME in the desert with what's shorn off. The letters are the size of lungs. Another person lights a fire nearby and the rest of the world is a planetarium families of rabbits jump up and down within. The person who lights the fire has six fingers on his right hand; when he points to a star he is pointing to the furthermost crackle his hand-bones make when they unfurl again to turn the coals. His extra finger has a life of its own. It points to the goat hair and forces me to knit a six-fingered glove. It points at me like a brain-dead twin and says *you are the one who turned all the sea birds into pieces of white cloth*. My foot is smack dab in the center of the fire, buried under a pile of hot coals. It is horrible, horrible pain. I knit pieces of the goat hair. I wonder if our baby is cold.

# WRITTEN FOR

*Do you think our attraction is joy or charity* you ask. Then you open your mouth and 12 mini-clowns drive off your tongue in their cars. You say *this is the only hemisphere in which one's sweaty palm is a clean thing, like a parquet floor*, then you make your way down the spiral staircase, hair in front of your eyes, pulling toothpick splinters from the roof of your mouth. A spiral staircase pulls us to the base of gravity until we are only multiples of pi.

# A SYSTEM OF MERMAIDS

You press your face against the tank, other boys fiddling with the Spirograph they have ready to go. *Is desire stronger than what causes a person to amputate herself* you ask. Coterminous, commingled, you nail yourself to a metallic bikini full of your best friend's eyes. You want to catch her breath on paper & think: *her breath her breath her breath her breath her breath on paper on paper on paper on paper on paper.*

# GIANT ATTRACTION WITH CREATURES

Everyone's tooth is
a little machine that can't

starfish itself to the lip
it loves. The way you speak

hits the ceiling & stays there
laryngitic, a blue noise

photoshopped clean I can't
stand so vertical. What brought

this image to light made a
motorcycle-growl & chicks

exploded from the eggs you
would have cracked into

my mouth. What brought this
image to light wrapped a

perfume ad around your hand
during the immaculate peeping

so you wave goodbye to infinity.

# RAZOR VOICE & THE SLEEPY

There is a summer cold
cut with something alive

when the curb fractures
into 1000 more.


From beekeeper hats


six onlooking children
stuff bread into ant holes

knowing everyone who does
goes blind.

# I AM AN ARCHEOLOGIST

When the skeleton of a man's "excuse me" finds

the primitive structure in ruins

beyond the clouds, I will have

some oatmeal or some pieces

of rubber on my face & I will be sorry.  To prove

I am God, I will step out of the ocean

to do the spooky dance.

# YOUR SIDEBURN AN IDAHO THAT GREW

The scent left a gray
furry feel I tried to save

in my hands. The storm
cantilevered you underneath

the cobbles, my legs
in the next neighborhood

ten feet long, dodging
harpsichords that fell from

the 5th floor like kisses. You
fell from the 5th floor like kisses.


I never told you
I walk around human

but have always been just a loose moon
rolling in the shadow

of a pony's belly—
a pony with ideas about falling

into a swimming pool of
the grayest, grayest furry feel

that never would be there.

OH OH OH

# SMOG

In the practice peephole a memory shook
the profane filament iris-echoing
its fault line. You spill symphonies trochaic
on a plate that doesn't exist, planed
below a hum a hundred minnows breathe salt to.
I am the empress bombing you. These kittens in my hand
take your hood to the balsam & scrape it.

## OH OH OH

Sparrow, I hold you with the scorpion's
noose, hold your old claw to the door

you dig. There is a raw fish on the calendar, it's
Monday, the rest of the garden fills with bird racket.

Hawks kite by, morph into old men. My disease is
uncivilized & moves limb to limb to puppet new

shockwaves. My naked leg cycles by
to the sounds of old men. My naked leg

finds a hammock & a black sheet & I ball
them up into a beehive in the shadows.

# RAIN CLOTHES & CUNEIFORM

Exemplar of dandelion trajectory, you make a hole
in my foot with your tactic. The game is a
someone-gets-the-pregnancy question. A child
lassoed your arm with his rope ladder, malignant of lip, but
will his eye flash before you rung to rung? A knife
about to marry its jailer slips from jaw when I make an air-body
with my hands. Do you notice the smoldering? Pendulums seed
their way to my mannerism like a dress hung on nothing.

# MAKE LIGHT

The sun's stabbed-

out eye parade, Dorothy,
apes the empty pick-up

I backfire from. I hate
no baby carriage lugged &

Oh Oh. Behind the permanent
tailgate blows one watt per dusk &

all over the shroud leftover light
webs out. Screen, pick up a

dollar, fifty fifty it & eat
a cracker dead. The new

slit on my arm spells out
*listen to the vultures make light*

*with their screams.* My leaf
foreshadows the

Victorian scarf you Oh
Oh Oh on my wrist

till the wound.

# MISERY DICTIONARY

Motor one meets motor two in a mannequin's
mouth. By the door what to get rid of creeps
over the toe the burnt light bulb bruises. I am a tower
plugged left to right by utility cords unable to wrap
my syllogism in the proper fable. Seven days of
spiders fill my tub with legs & I take
my scarf to enscarf you, Sergeant. I take to the park a dozen
dogs. Where is the water lily in your throat
I memorized? Where is the half-black sky wedging you
into dove-smashed glass? In the morning, your dead father
swelters in the window with handfuls of plant food
& people stand in line to see. After 3 years I call
when the grieving children bake-sale, better
actors for it. *Would you touch me* was the last wing-swish bleeding
from your voice in the swamp you dared to touch. In the book was
a black leather boot we wore at the same time & wouldn't
tear off. Here is my misery dictionary. Here is my
space noise. And the lambs who wait silently fold their hooves
in the garden below.

# MAGIC PHOTON

I cry my beasts home one
by one. In the belly I cry
my beasts a photon
& cry & cry my photon.
In the belly my scorpion's
beasty eye will two
times cry a crystal to
beasty beasty me.

# FIVE STAR

Not even lamps will behave you, known
as the song sandwich. Did you notice

we never asked a question? A question?
So-called clock, lose that ugly narc, please

lose that ugly narc & lose that ugly narc.

# BANDIT

A nail through sugar
67 inches away inches

remoras toward
your breakfast claw.

67 of me take your
hoof off between

a carbon-eaten rail &
relax a single neuron

to its grape.

# INTERIORIZE

I am not the white
5:55 many doves pearl out

from your eyelid. A
blue factory lips lipless

the soft worn I
the bone makes

after she eats
ephemera seven

times to pat
her name down.

# RED MOVIE

Shy lanterns wipe bugs, shot in the filament
with a truck driver's BB fresh from paralyzing
squirrels. No one should take no one by the throat.
No one should turn someone into. This
is how we kiss: by the river at knife-point,
blue eye laser-feeding the bit of air
stewed so long in its grass fever. Sitting
in shallow water where the carp swim
breath-starved like capsules. The oxygen affinity of carp blood.
The eye of girl to fish, dead on a tennis racket
spilling eggs. Who vanishes in the tree shadow just before
a root opens his foot & the only voice he fires out dies?

# SHE TURNED INTO

Table underling, enshroud
the hand I cut

off at the root so you
can live a normal-man life.

# BLUSH

We serpentine as walk-
chemistry would have

eaten a ball of snared wife
for your white lunch. To sew

your eye back in I will someday
say to this day I can't tell which

one it was it was grown over with
roots you pushed a vision of into

the hologram, only the hollow
piece of cauldron we bruised on

but never named still bites.

# IN SEARCH OF FACES IN
# THE DEAD OF NIGHT

|

Chickens roost in satellite dishes down the hill from this village you love. Cinderblock shacks row by row crack in half and a wrecking ball finishes them off. You shepherd the mini-horses through the rubble. Why your knees and their knees buckle all at once while I wait at the edge of the water I can't put my finger on.

By the edge of the water one cargo truck crashes into the home with the best sea view and now there is a man inside the truck selling chicken necks two lira a handful. I look at my watch and he says to me *Victoria, Victoria, take my hands, please please take my hands.* Wild dogs choke on Styrofoam near the front tire.

Your beard follows me, rests on my shoulder, follows me, but you are stuck on the ridge in the rubble, with all of those horse eyes blinking. *We deserve a blank beach where we can touch each other without death* you say to them.

I don't know if I am Victoria. I eat small pieces of concrete in my cereal and take morphine for the lump in my throat. If I am Victoria, in the middle of my heart is a tiny, dirty beak.

The ocean ripped your pants down and clamped onto your neck just down the road from that Mexican place by the tomb you like. You ate an eyeball on your dinner fish. You ate an eyeball on your dinner fish. Here is my milk bowl the temperature of skin. Here is the bag of ink to replace your blood, a fort of towels to mop up the horse tears coming out of your eyes. It is full of awesome drugs to yawn you alive. You are 95 wheels curling faster than a fisherman's fist.

11

A big red bird selects its own sky and its own big red planet to plunge a beak through while two half-bodied, blue ladies stare from a bluer corner holding cups of tea until one pokes the other's face with a twig and hits instead an outer Zulu mask. *Pardon me, Gladys,* the first one says. Her friend's eyes nod back from behind some straw fringe.

The horned black animal in the forest out the window drinks coke from a gourd against a tree next to a sack of arrows.

I would paint your hands blue, too, Gladys, to make them corpse-like, then I would guide your teacup back into place.

I stare at you and say flat out: *I owe sadness my life*. At the last word, *life*, a layer forms over my face & the black animal splits into three birds. Out of a fifth-story window it falls in thirds, unable to get those wings going.

*Because the birds are not birds they are mothers giving birth*, you say, *they are sad decorations made of old potato. They are teapots with eyes made of old potato.*

All I know is when my mask is against the glass I can still reach back to touch the little garden of petunias in your kitchen sink. When I reach back I can touch everything about you before 10,000 colors get stuck under the fake lips my real lips press against.

I sit here with an erased face trying to get to the boat: the only boat under the only cloud under the only planet. My friend understands that the more I run in figure eights, the more the river thins to little pieces of straw. You know the famous saying: The cat who can't reach the liver says *oh, dammit.* There is a small wire from my brain to my asshole making me run faster but all I see in front of my eyes is horses with small heads bleeding from the knees.

There was a time when people ate pudding and wore beaver skin pelts. I saw you there with much blacker hair, hiding behind a cactus full of bullet holes. You left the broom on the roof two million times and started painting pictures of jesters. The reason I know you did this is that when you threw your paintbrush out the window it hit me square in the wooden cheek. Then I stared into your bedroom for 45 days, watched you smoke hash and pull a drunk girl's pants down over and over. You smiled so devilishly. You winked so goddamnishly. I will tell you I know the secret to painting corpse hands and the secret to cutting them off.

# ORPHANS

# ORPHANS

My face so haloed by charred
orphans you have never

seen. When we arrest our
mouths, instant half-hearts

fizzle from each eye. I take
a picture of you with my

throat & years hatch a version
never touched by light

that will make it real. Same
goes for the nest I park you in

& your arm shaped as if slung
over logs: I don't know

whether to freeze or crawl
into the picture it becomes.

# INVENTION OF ONE MINUTE

Over mountain tips
hours drop

ugly marbles. Those
aliens in my throat

have no happy-to-see-
you look until you

cut me open.

# SUPERCONTINENT

You, ear to the little
boy's hand, tell him

someone is waiting
in a fort for you.

I take a fountain
photo & chew on

my cocktail sword, claw
off a piece of shoe &

throw it at a man
making molehills

of his napkin. I feel
my freckles fall off.

The airplane
murdered one look

at your blue shirt &
hushed. I was

made to find it, to walk
straight through to your

bone field.

# THE QUESTION BEHAVES ITS WAY

An ice swarm grows
dinosaur-eyed if you've seen

the sad living girl. If you know
she's dead you know she's open-

jawed letting a whole
slab in, so wake up in a sprint

to the water, fevery
& draw huge jesters on her lip.

# LAG

A fort of black togas buries
one Pangea & some blue

blows from rearview. Someone
asks where the flower I put on

went & I say I'd rather smell
like Pangea, then I scream *Pangea!*

when the sun razes my
driver arm, when the small

cloak I stick in your heart
as a cushion loses its

pinhole on the world.

# SLOWLY DEFORMS AND SLOWS GRAVITY

I feel a month ice
over, leave the

stuck cat in its
grate & hear some if its

meows come off
your suit. A palace

moves into a hole
in the mountain

coke numbs
lips we hear

moving by
the lime-wedge

bag. This is
where we live &

where our babies
tooth.  Years back

we made an airport's
worth of dead

whales line up to
cloak us with washing

machine hearts. It
was father's day &

the babies didn't
know your name.

# THEORIES OF A DROPPED PLANETARIUM

Took out a camera & every inch
happened when the monitor changed.

Every time I saw you in my air, a
question veined out in the rearview.

What kind of ulcer grew when
a kid borrowed your cell phone &

suctioned his sunglasses to your eye?
This weather left leather with it,

invisible offspring treading past.

# VIEW FROM A BLACK FORT

The minute a minute is un-invented
I will show the blank photo of it, every

naked inch cramped in a wet heart-box
under the seat, the red shine of your

first word gliding up & down chambers
having stunned children to laugh

attacks after pulling their mothers'
varnished faces from the mud.

# UPPER WEST

Turtle pond, the baby
girls wake Russianly

& jealous, a dead kite
is wind-hidden.

She & she estrange
the city effervescent

under its bench.


When my phone
rings a blond

hologram holy,
your t-shirt

offs, the rooftop
pops a firework

of blueberry
teeterings you take

pictures of. I put
my pants on, drop

my phone in.



You are off
to run your bodega

hand over the limes
but my arm stuck

to the other hand
makes a tissue nest

for every dead fish.

This origami-
crumpled blind

spot a concrete
sun in front

of you burned
so you could

no longer
make out.


Turtles nudge
mud, around the

corner hellos
from twin phones

repeat to no ear
till specks on

the horizon.

This is why I'm selling
everything paired—

little nests from
your eyelashes, fire

bundles each
lung bled.


I wilt when echoes
distinguish

their source, when
ears go stereo in vain.

# STORM

Our tree-place leaks, a shudder
whites the heartbeat in my foot &

each small lined-up canoe whips away
so that when our oar-swirls meet, a

tornado stirs the whole brotherhood
& even the sun goes tornado. The park

as people run around it, earmuffed, liquefies
to kill the thunderbolt zagging from your tongue.

# ROOF

Came back one time
to see what breakfast is

starving. When I down
a vodka in two hammock

swings you clap. I put a shrimp
on your tongue when you won't.

Shut up you say with
your jaw about your radio-

silent friend who mailed
pink photos of a baby & slipped

*This is my law school* in on
rolling paper. What am I

doing when you fill two whole
rolls with sunset & hand me

a third I lockbox shut. In his
envelope were also some ashes.

# WHAT REPLACES US WHEN WE GO

They found our pearls
now they know thy east

village feet. They know
thy feet I do with

Swedish drink & sonic
milk. I bathe in mother's

youth, watch my Lifetime.
They send some arrest

warrants to her so why
be a no-show

hacking through
shadows to figure.

# QUEENS

You sicken on the air
mattress & mimic

three kinds of
morning left fractured

in the back drain's
dove-shrine, then warp

into a whole gang
of babies. *I won't*

*eat meat on the porch*
screaming, you say

smoking, then reach
your fennel hands

over to top-knot
my hair. My hips are

your handlebar so tell
me what size & tell

me there's static in this.

••••••

# ACTIVITY FOR TWO

Your bifurcated body leap-frogs
the whole orchard & lands torso-up

in a pool I found. I hear the sound
whenever your tinny skirt upends:

a Wednesday-squeal like the month's
first siren. When the ringing stops

you split in half all the way & six orbs
appear in the grass in place of you, silver

in a perfect row, as though offsprung
from trees in the grove, fruit-quiet

or mouse-hole-quiet
by the twilight we sift through

safely bathing-capped. I know something
we can do together when your legs

come back: file the sharp cliff down
to a buffed little ramp & jet each orb

toward the vertical nooks
we footprint over the cliff dust.

# BAREFOOT

In my bikini it's all I do all day. Seek
the source of the siren I hear

till paralyzed when you go-go dance
or practice rocket-tennis with the erectile

launcher. In that regard, I am a lifeguard
other men can't understand. I look around

to find out if they hear it too
but every man is already in his invisi-suit

ready for the sun to split into sixths.
Every man is running around making breath-

stroke gestures in his invisi-suit.
I'm alone with the sound either way,

and more slouchy the further I walk.

# MONSIEUR

Tracing your movements in the grove is the only thing
that doesn't bore me, which is why I swim

so poorly.  I had a dream your mouth
opened & the noise got thicker—

there were baby antennae sprouting
from the base of each tree. It was then you

convinced me we should split into sixths
together & wait for the sun to raid us.

# MME.

Do you know a thing called scream
was programmed into your head-

medicine accidentally? That is why you
swim so poorly. Little bits of seed

came out in the swimming pool that
were stuck behind the stripe in your

speedo. It starts with my hands. Circles
appear on the tops of my wrists, and I

freeze & drop the racket. This is called
an orgasm. They happen in sixes,

fives, fours, threes, twos, ones &
zeros. I tried to megaphone it before

I disappeared, but my scream
was sliced off with an invisible knife.

# LEISURE ACTIVITY

I know something we can do
together. We can just lean our

heads back like this to the wall
where our voices won't register

eye to eye. When we vanish
a white field will roll out

where poolwater used to be
& the hem of the grove

will quiver like someone cut it
out of the landscape & threw it

up high to cover the
top of the sun. See how good

that feels on our throats.
Men take pictures of us

glowing & we never know it.

# VACATION SPOT

My open mouth-malfunction
the pitch may finally have seized

to let a secret drip out into
our kind of skin, the kind of

skin that makes your head
paralytic & dermal-coded

when the circles appear. You said
*The siren is just nerves headed somewhere*

*to explode* & I knew you had watched
a kidnapper throw a red-shoed

girl into the fake ocean. It made
you sad right down to the photon.

I know a vacation spot for when
your hand clenches shut &

we morph into orbs, finished.

# FIN

Electro-kinetically I am moving
against you when seed-like

up the building at sunset we
travel & turn from silver fruit

to fire beads below one tree
sprouting up far from the grove

to soft sounds of sheep-murmur
on the yellowest day of the month.

# LOVE-LOVE

The wind wants language. I could
stare at you until the wind grows ears.

If it's about what replaces us when we go
there may be traces here & over there

where cotton patterns spill. Two ironies
of this type of death are love-love

at expiration & hard layers
of calcium archeologists will poke at

for years where each ball is stuck.
You know I ate stars by the handful

while crying for the deaths
of the rest of the Kings.

# STAR SIREN

A fitness I couldn't whistle came
movie-formed, pulsing body parts

I didn't recognize. Only one of us
survived & now I am stuck

worshipping. Do you know what
it's like to have a white dwarf

inside your chest? Do you know
to search for the scar?

# ACKNOWLEDGEMENTS

Poems from this manuscript first appeared in the following journals:

*Saltgrass*
*Fou*
*Octopus Magazine*
*Left-Facing Bird*
*Omnidawn Feature*
*Rooms Outlast Us*
*751 Magazine*
*Handsome*

# NOTES

"In Search of Faces…" arrived after a viewing of the paintings of Melih Özuysal.

● ● ● ● ● ● is loosely based on the film *The Ataraxians* by Sabine Gruffaut and Ben Russell. Set in Southern France in the future, the film depicts the death of the leisure class and "what replaces them when they go."